W9-AAL-674

salads

hot and cold

TRIDENT PRESS
INTERNATIONAL

Published by:
TRIDENT PRESS INTERNATIONAL
801. 12th Avenue South
Suite 400
Naples, FL 34102 U.S.A.
Copyright(c) Trident Press
Tel: (239) 649 7077
Fax: (239) 649 5832
Email: tridentpress@worldnet.att.net
Website: www.trident-international.com

acknowledgements

Salads Hot and Cold
Compiled by: R&R Publications Marketing P/L
Creative Director: Paul Sims
Production Manager: Anthony Carroll
Food Photography: Warren Webb

Food Stylists: Di Kirby, Wendy Berecry
Recipe Development: Ellen Argyriou,
Sheryle Eastwood, Kim Freedman,
Lucy Kelly, Donna Hay, Anneka Mitchell,
Penelope Peel, Jody Vassallo,
Belinda Warn, Loukie Werle.
Proof Reader: Andrea Hazell-Tarttelin

*All rights reserved. No part of this book may
be stored, reproduced or transmitted in any
form or by any means without written
permission of the publisher, except in the case
of brief quotations embodied in critical articles
and reviews.*

Includes Index
ISBN 1 58279464 2
EAN 9 781582 79464 8
UPC 6 15269 94642 8

Second Edition 2003
*Computer Typeset in Humanist 521
& Times New Roman*

Printed in Colombia

contents

introduction

introduction

In this book you will find many delightful surprises, especially for those who thought that salads could only be served on a hot summer's day, and for those, too, who imagine a salad to be the usual greenery served time and time again.

Salads need not have a special season; simple, easy-to-prepare green salads with a special dressing or mixed vegetable salads make wonderful accompaniments to meats, chicken, fish, omelettes and quiches at any time of the year.

Whole or torn, leaves add colour and flavour to salads. Shredded, or shaped into cups for individual portions, they also play an important supporting role in the presentation of cold dishes made with other vegetables, meat, poultry or fish.

The secret to a successful salad is simple: always choose fresh, unblemished salad ingredients, then prepare them in an imaginative way. Combine flavours and textures of salad ingredients carefully and always complement your salads with a compatible dressing or mayonnaise.

We know you will enjoy the salads presented in this book. You will find that the recipes contain a variety of ingredients but are simple to prepare.

Fine food comes in many guises, but seldom is it as convenient, flavoursome or healthful as when it is gathered from the garden or garnered from a greengrocer with garden-fresh produce.

Fresh fruits and vegetables are relatively inexpensive, easy to prepare and full of fibre and nutrients. They come in a glorious array of colours, offer a wide range of tastes and textures and provide raw energy on a sustained level, unlike the quick gratification offered by sugary snacks.

Small wonder that salads — whether simple or carefully composed — are becoming more and more a staple of our daily diet. It is so easy to introduce raw foods in the form of a salad, either at the start of meal, as an accompaniment or, in the French fashion, as a separate course served after the main and before the dessert (to cleanse the palate and, equally importantly, to avoid any conflict between the dressing and the wine). A hearty main-course salad can be a meal in itself, at any season. If you've never sampled a warm salad, now's the time to experience the contrast in textures and temperatures offered by Warm Steak Salad with Pawpaw and Spanish Onion. And, while Fruit salads are conventionally served as desserts, recipes like Melon and Onion Salad also make excellent savouries.

This comprehensive collection includes over a hundred recipes for salads of every description, plus dozens of dressings.

knowing
your greens

In recent years the availability of various types of salad vegetables has increased so much that a trip to the greengrocer or fruit and vegetable section of any supermarket can be mind-boggling. Use the following as a guide to help you identify, and know how best to use, some of those exotic-looking salad greens.

Witloof or Chicory

Sometimes called Brussels chicory or Belgian endive, this vegetable can be eaten raw or cooked. It has tightly clustered, smooth, white leaves with greenish yellow tips and looks somewhat like an oblong tight-headed lettuce. Witloof means 'white leaf' and when buying this vegetable always look for the whitest witloof. Slightly bitter in taste, it is a versatile vegetable that combines well with a range of flavours.

Curly Endive

Another member of the chicory family, curly endive has large, curly, frilly-edged leaves with a slightly bitter flavour. The leaves graduate from a pale, green yellow to dark green. Use the paler heart leaves and stalks. Sold in large bunches, curly endive makes an attractive bed for a meat or chicken salad and is an interesting addition to a mixed green salad.

Butter or Round Lettuce

There are a several varieties of butter lettuce which include Bibb, Boston and Butterhead. The one thing they have in common is that they are a soft, smallish lettuce with a mild flavour. Often grown hydroponically, the butter lettuce lacks the crunch of iceberg or cos, but is popular in mixed lettuce salads.

Cos or Romaine Lettuce

Popular with the Romans, this lettuce was named by them because they claim to have discovered it on the Greek island of Cos. Later the English and Europeans renamed it Romaine lettuce after the Romans. Today it is known by both names depending on where in the world you reside. This lettuce has an elongated head of dark green oval leaves and a crisp pale green heart. It has a pungent flavour and stays crisp. Its main claim to fame is its use in the traditional Caesar Salad.

Iceberg or Crisp Head Lettuce

Probably the most popular and well known of lettuces, the iceberg lettuce is a large lettuce with crisp outer leaves and a firm, sweet heart. It is the basis of many salads as it combines well with other lettuces and salad greens.

Red Leaf Lettuces

These are among the prettiest of lettuces and include mignonette, lollo rosso and red oakleaf. They are characterised by their soft, smallish leaves with pink to red tinged edges. These lettuces have a delicate sweet flavour. The red leaf lettuces are usually interchangeable in a recipe and more often than not are used to give a salad colour and interest.

Radicchio

Yet another member of the chicory family, the radicchio is beetroot-coloured with white veins and has a tightly packed head. It has a tangy, slightly bitter flavour and is a much loved salad vegetable in Italy where it is called red chicory. In Italy, radicchio is the name generally used for chicory.

Rocket

Also known as arugula, roquette and rugula, this plant has small, peppery, dark green leaves and should be used while still young. Rocket first grew wild in the Mediterranean area and was a popular salad green with the ancient Romans. Still rare in many areas, it is in fact easy to grow and for something different in your salads, it is well worth the effort.

English Spinach or Spinach

The young, fresh, dark green leaves of this vegetable are delicious eaten raw. One of the most popular spinach salads consists of roughly torn spinach leaves, crisp bacon pieces and croutons, with a dressing made from the cooking juices of the bacon, lemon juice and freshly ground black pepper.

Watercress

Watercress has smooth round leaves, crunchy stems and a pungent, slightly peppery flavour. Use young outer leaves and tender stems for salads. The remainder can be used in soups. Watercress has long been used as both a food and a medicine and can be traced back to the ancient Greeks. It combines well with other milder salad greens and is popular as a garnish for salads and open sandwiches. Watercress does not keep well and should be stored upright in the refrigerator in a container of water, and covered with a plastic food bag. Change the water daily for to ensure lasting freshness.

salad
vegetables

While lettuce, chicory and a variety of other greens form the basis of many salads, there are also a number of other salad vegetables which are popular and should not be forgotten when creating wonderful salads.

Cabbage

One of the oldest cultivated vegetable species, the cabbage family includes white cabbage, red cabbage and yellow and green savoy cabbage. Used raw and finely shredded, it is the basis of the ever popular coleslaw. Red cabbage, usually cooked, is also delicious raw, and when shredded and combined with green cabbage makes an attractive slaw. Store cabbage in a plastic food bag in the crisper section of the refrigerator.

Red, green or yellow capsicum

Also called peppers and bell peppers, when sliced or chopped these add colour and crunch to salads. Always choose well-shaped, firm capsicums with a glossy, smooth skin. Dull-looking capsicums, those with soft spots and wrinkled skins should be avoided. Remove the stalk, seeds and white membrane before use. Roasted capsicum also make an interesting salad garnish. Capsicums should keep in the crisper section of the refrigerator for 5-7 days.

Celery

Use either sliced, cut into sticks or as celery curls (see Techniques section). The leaves also make a tasty and attractive salad garnish.

Cucumber

The variety of cucumbers available include apple, green or ridge, Lebanese and telegraph cucumber. The green or ridge and telegraph cucumbers are the most widely available. To prepare cucumbers you need only peel them if the skin is tough or bitter as leaving the skin on is said to help with digestion. Cucumbers (except the apple variety) should have bright green skins with a firm, fresh appearance. Apple cucumbers should have a pale yellow-white skin.

Onion

All types of onions can be used raw in salads. White and brown onions have a strong, hot, pungent taste and should be used sparingly. The red onion is a mild sweet onion that adds a pretty colour to any salad. Spring onions, also known as scallions or green onions, give a mild fresh onion flavour. Use onions either sliced or chopped in salads or as a garnish.

Radishes

These small, crisp red bulbs can be used whole, sliced, chopped or grated in salads. Select radishes with fresh-looking leaves and bright-coloured bulbs.

Sprouts

There are a number of sprout varieties available, the most popular being alfalfa and bean sprouts. To save wastage, you might like to grow your own sprouts – see Sprouting Know-how. Sprouts should be kept in a plastic food bag or the container in which you purchased them.

Tomatoes

Tomatoes should have a good red colour and firm flesh. Used whole or halved, cherry and the small, yellow teardrop tomatoes are also popular salad ingredients. For best flavour, tomatoes should always be used at room temperature.

Hydroponically grown lettuces last longer as they are still growing when you buy them and will continue to grow if kept in a plastic food bag in the crisper section of the refrigerator. Many varieties are now grown hydroponically making them available all year round.

Lettuce should be stored in the vegetable crisper section of your refrigerator. Place the whole lettuce in a plastic food bag or covered container. Separate leaves and wash just prior to using.

Always remember to wash salad vegetables before using. To prepare lettuce, cut out the core using a stainless steel knife, then separate leaves and wash briefly in cold water. Dry the leaves by shaking off the excess water, then pat dry with a teatowel. The leaves can also be drained in a colander or salad basket, or use a salad spinner or centrifugal dryer (a piece of equipment especially designed for drying lettuce leaves). Always dress a lettuce salad as close to serving time as possible. The longer the dressing sits on the leaves the less crisp they will be.

chilli noodle salad

veggie
salads

A sensational salad can add colour,

*flavour and variety to an otherwise simple meal.
Many of these easy salads can also double
as light meals. What more delicious meal
could there be than a Roasted Vegetable Salad
served with crusty bread and a glass wine?*

chargrilled
vegetable salad

Method:

1 Brush sweet corn cobs, eggplant (aubergines), red capsicum (peppers), zucchini (courgettes) and leeks with olive oil. Place vegetables on a preheated hot barbecue and cook, turning occasionally, for 15 minutes or until vegetables are golden and tender.

2 To make dressing, place basil, rosemary, chilli oil and vinegar in a screwtop jar and shake well to combine. Drizzle dressing over warm vegetables.

Note: Smoky flavoured, crisp on the outside and tender within, char-grilled vegetables taste quite unlike any other. You may substitute the proportions of vegetables listed here if any of them are in short supply.

Serves 6

ingredients

2 cobs fresh sweet corn, cut into 3 cm/1¼ in pieces
6 baby eggplant (aubergines), halved lengthwise
3 red capsicums (peppers), cut into quarters
6 zucchini (courgettes), halved lengthwise
6 small leeks, halved lengthwise
olive oil
Herb dressing
2 tablespoons chopped fresh basil
1 tablespoon chopped fresh rosemary or 1 teaspoon dried rosemary
2 tablespoons chilli oil
2 tablespoons balsamic vinegar

marinated
eggplant salad

Method:

1 Place eggplant (aubergines) in a colander, sprinkle with salt and drain for 20 minutes. Rinse eggplant (aubergines) under cold water and pat dry with absorbent kitchen paper.

2 Preheat barbecue to a high heat. Brush eggplant (aubergine) slices with oil, place on barbecue grill and cook for 2 minutes each side or until tender and golden. Place in a shallow dish.

3 To make dressing, place onion, parsley, basil, chilli, vinegar and black pepper to taste in a screwtop jar and shake to combine. Pour dressing over eggplant (aubergines) and toss. Cover and marinate in the refrigerator for at least 1 hour before serving.

Note: This salad can be marinated for up to 24 hours. Salting eggplant (aubergine) degorges it of any bitter juices. For this recipe, it also ensures that you do not end up with excess juices coming out during marinating.

Serves 8

ingredients

3 large eggplant (aubergines), sliced
sea salt
2-3 tablespoons olive oil
Herb and balsamic dressing
1 red onion, sliced
2 tablespoons chopped fresh flat-leaf parsley
2 tablespoons chopped fresh basil
1 fresh green chilli, seeded and finely chopped
2/3 cup/170ml/5½fl oz balsamic vinegar
freshly ground black pepper

Oven temperature 220°C, 425°F, Gas 7

moroccan
vegetable salad

Method:
1 *To make marinade, place turmeric, cumin, cinnamon, harissa, garlic, oil, lime juice and honey in a glass or ceramic bowl and whisk to combine.*
2 *Add onions, garlic, carrots, fennel, parsnips and sweet potatoes to marinade and toss to coat. Cover and marinate in the refrigerator for 2-3 hours.*
3 *To make herbed yoghurt, place yoghurt, dill, mint and black pepper to taste in a bowl and mix to combine. Cover and refrigerate until required.*
4 *Transfer vegetables and marinade to a baking dish and bake for 1 hour or until vegetables are tender. Serve hot or warm with herbed yoghurt.*
Note: *Harissa is a hot chilli paste used in North African cooking. It is available from specialty food shops or you can make a simple version yourself by combining 2 tablespoons each of chilli powder, ground cumin, tomato paste (purée) and olive oil with 1 teaspoon salt.*
Serves 4

ingredients

10 baby onions, peeled
10 cloves garlic, peeled
3 carrots, cut into 5cm/2in lengths
1 bulb fennel, cut into wedges
4 parsnips, cut into quarters, lengthwise
500g/1 lb sweet potatoes, cut into
2cm/³/4in thick rounds
<u>Spicy lime marinade</u>
1 teaspoon ground turmeric
1 teaspoon ground cumin
1 teaspoon ground cinnamon
¹/2 teaspoon harissa
2 cloves garlic, crushed
¹/2 cup/125ml/4fl oz olive oil
3 tablespoons lime juice
1 tablespoon honey
<u>Herbed yoghurt</u>
1 cup/200g/6¹/2oz natural yogurt
2 tablespoons chopped fresh dill
2 tablespoons chopped fresh mint
freshly ground black pepper

gado gado

Method:

1 To make sauce, heat oil in a frying pan over a medium heat, add onion and chilli and cook, stirring, for 3 minutes or until onion is soft. Stir in peanut butter, coriander, coconut cream, kechap manis and chilli sauce and stirring, bring to the boil. Reduce heat and simmer for 5 minutes, then stir in sugar and lemon juice. Cool slightly. The sauce should be slightly runny, if it is too thick add a little water.

2 Boil, steam or microwave beans and carrots, separately, until they are bright green and bright orange, then rinse under cold running water and drain well.

3 Heat oil in a frying pan or wok over a high heat, add tofu and stir-fry until golden. Drain on absorbent kitchen paper and cool slightly.

4 To serve, arrange piles of beans, carrots, tofu, red capsicum (pepper), cucumbers, mushrooms and eggs on a large serving platter. Serve with sauce.

Note: Kechap manis is a thick sweet seasoning sauce used in Indonesian cooking. It is sometimes called Indonesian soy sauce. If unavailable, a mixture of soy sauce and dark corn syrup or golden syrup can be used in its place.

Serves 6

ingredients

125g/4oz green beans, sliced lengthwise
2 carrots, cut into thick strips
2 tablespoons vegetable oil
185g/6oz firm tofu, cut into thick strips
1 large red capsicum (pepper), cut into thick strips
2 cucumbers, cut into thick strips
12 small button mushrooms
6 hard-boiled eggs, cut into wedges
<u>Peanut Sauce</u>
1 tablespoon peanut (groundnut) oil
1 onion, finely chopped
1 fresh red chilli, finely chopped
2/3 cup/170g/5 1/2oz peanut butter
1 tablespoon ground coriander
3/4 cup/185ml/6fl oz coconut cream
3 tablespoons kechap manis
2 teaspoons chilli sauce
1 teaspoon palm or brown sugar
1 tablespoon lemon juice

Oven temperature 180°C, 350°F, Gas 4

roasted
vegetable salad

Method:

1 *Place fennel, sweet potatoes and shallots in a nonstick baking dish and spray with olive oil. Sprinkle with cumin seeds and bake for 30-35 minutes or until vegetables are soft and golden. Set aside to cool for 10-15 minutes or until vegetables are warm.*

2 *Place vegetables in a serving bowl, add beans, rocket, cheese, vinegar and black pepper to taste and toss.*

Note: *The shallots used in this recipe are the French échalote. If unavailable red or yellow shallots used in Asian cooking or pickling onions can be used instead.*

Serves 4

ingredients

3 bulbs fennel, cut into wedges
2 sweet potatoes, peeled and chopped
12 shallots, peeled
olive oil spray
1 teaspoon cumin seeds
315g/10oz green beans, blanched
185g/6oz rocket leaves
155g/5oz reduced-fat feta cheese, chopped
2-3 tablespoons balsamic vinegar
freshly ground black pepper

out
of the fire salad

Method:

1 Place tomatoes, cut side up, and garlic on a baking tray. Brush tomatoes with chilli oil and sprinkle with salt and black pepper to taste. Bake for 45-50 minutes or until the tomatoes are deep red in colour and semi-dried - take care not to overcook or they will loose their moisture. Set aside until garlic is cool enough to handle, then peel.

2 Place tomatoes, garlic, chickpeas, artichokes, olives, onion and basil in a bowl and toss gently to combine.

3 Combine rocket and Parmesan cheese and arrange on a serving platter, top with tomato mixture and hard-boiled eggs. Combine vinegar and olive oil and drizzle over salad.

Note: For perfect hard-boiled eggs, tightly pack the eggs into a saucepan, pointed end down, cover with cold water and bring to the boil. Boil for 10 minutes. Drain eggs and cool under cold running water. This method for boiling eggs ensures that there is no dark ring around the yolk and that it is centred.

Serves 4 as a main meal or 6 as a light meal

Oven temperature 180°C, 350°F, Gas 4

ingredients

12 plum (egg or Italian) tomatoes, halved
1 bulb garlic, divided into cloves and left unpeeled
1-2 tablespoons chilli oil
sea salt
freshly ground black pepper
440g/14oz canned chickpeas, rinsed and drained
185g/6oz marinated artichokes, quartered
125g/4oz marinated black olives
1 red onion, sliced
3 tablespoons shredded fresh basil
1 bunch rocket
125g/4oz fresh Parmesan cheese, shaved
6 hard-boiled eggs, halved
2 tablespoons balsamic vinegar
2 tablespoons extra virgin olive oil

sweet
chilli potato salad

Method:

1 Halve or quarter potatoes, depending on their size, place in a baking dish, drizzle with oil and toss to coat. Bake for 40 minutes or until crisp and golden.

3 Reduce oven temperature to 180°C/ 350°F/ Gas 4, then pour chilli sauce over potatoes and bake for 10-15 minutes or until the chilli sauce begins to caramelise, take care that it does not burn.

3 Transfer potatoes to a bowl, add spring onions and mint and toss gently. Serve topped with yogurt and scattered with peanuts.

Note: Sweet chilli sauce is available from Oriental food shops and most supermarkets.

Serves 6

ingredients

1 ½ kg/3 lb baby new potatoes
3 tablespoons olive oil
½ cup/125ml/4fl oz sweet chilli sauce
4 spring onions, sliced
2 tablespoons finely shredded fresh mint
3 tablespoons natural yoghurt
60g/2oz peanuts, roasted

roasted
capsicums with herbs

Photograph opposite

roasted peppers with herbs

ingredients

3 red capsicums (peppers)
2 green capsicums(peppers)
4 medium fresh green chillies
2 onions, quartered
2 tablespoons fresh marjoram leaves
2 tablespoons fresh thyme leaves
¹/₄ cup/60ml/2fl oz lime juice
¹/₄ cup/60ml/2fl oz olive oil
freshly ground black pepper

Method:

1 *Place red and green capsicums (peppers) and chillies in a hot frying pan or comal and cook until skins are blistered and charred. Place capsicums (peppers) and chillies in a plastic food bag and stand for 10 minutes or until cool enough to handle.*

2 *Carefully remove skins from capsicums (peppers) and chillies, then cut off tops and remove seeds and membranes. Cut into thick slices.*

3 *Place onions in frying pan or comal and cook for 5 minutes or until soft and charred.*

4 *Place capsicum (peppers), chillies, onions, marjoram, thyme, lime juice, oil and black pepper to taste in a bowl and toss to combine. Stand for 30 minutes before serving.*

Note: *A comal is a steel, cast iron or unglazed earthenware cooking disk, which is used for cooking and heating tortillas and for toasting other ingredients such as chillies and pumpkin seeds.* **Serves 6**

tomato
salad

Method:
1 Place egg (plum or Italian) tomatoes, cherry tomatoes, tomatoes, onion, vinegar, basil and black pepper to taste in a bowl and toss to combine. Set aside to stand for 30 minutes.
2 Line a large serving platter with lettuce leaves and top with tomato mixture.
   Note: This salad can be made using any combination of tomatoes - so check the market and use what is in season and available.
   Serves 6

ingredients

**6 egg (plum or Italian) tomatoes,
cut into wedges
250g/8oz cherry tomatoes, halved
3 seasonal tomatoes, sliced
1 red onion, chopped
2 tablespoons red wine vinegar
2 tablespoons chopped fresh basil
freshly ground black pepper
assorted lettuce leaves**

warm
vegetable salad

Method:

1 To make vinaigrette, place olive oil, vinegar, thyme, sugar and black pepper to taste in a screwtop jar and shake well to combine. Set aside.

2 Heat 2 teaspoons vegetable oil in a wok over a high heat, add hazelnuts and stir-fry for 3 minutes. Set aside. Heat remaining oil in wok, add onions and stir-fry for 3 minutes or until golden.

3 Add carrots, zucchini (courgettes), snow peas (mangetout), mushrooms, green and red capsicums (peppers), spring onions and asparagus and stir-fry for 5 minutes. Return hazelnuts to wok, add vinaigrette and toss to combine.

Note: A heavy wok made of carbon steel will give better cooking results than a stainless steel or aluminium one.

Serves 4

ingredients

1 tablespoon vegetable oil
125g/4oz blanched hazelnuts
2 onions, chopped
2 carrots, sliced
2 zucchini (courgettes), chopped
155g/5oz snow peas (mangetout)
4 field mushrooms, sliced
1 green capsicum (pepper), sliced
1 red capsicum (pepper), sliced
6 spring onions, chopped
250g/8oz asparagus, halved
Red Wine and Thyme Vinaigrette
¹/₃ cup/90ml/3fl oz olive oil
¹/₄ cup/60ml/2fl oz red wine vinegar
1 tablespoons chopped fresh thyme
1 teaspoon sugar
freshly ground black pepper

Oven temperature 200°C, 400°F, Gas 6

green
salad in creamy dressing

Method:

1 Cook bacon in a frying pan over a medium heat for 4-5 minutes or until crisp. Remove bacon from pan and drain on absorbent kitchen paper until cool.

2 Arrange lettuces, tomatoes, carrots, celery, snow peas (mangetout) and bacon on a serving platter or in a large salad bowl.

3 To make dressing, place mayonnaise, sour cream, lemon juice and black pepper to taste in a bowl and mix to combine. Drizzle dressing over salad, cover and chill until required.

Serves 10

ingredients

6 rashers bacon, chopped
2 lettuces of your choice, leaves separated and torn into pieces
250g/8oz cherry tomatoes, halved
2 carrots, cut into strips
2 sticks celery, cut into strips
125g/4oz snow peas (mangetout)
Creamy dressing
1/2 cup/125g/4oz mayonnaise
1/2 cup/125g/4oz sour cream
1 tablespoon lemon juice
freshly ground black pepper

marinated
tomato salad

Method:

1 *Place tomatoes, cheese, onion and basil in a bowl and toss to combine.*
2 *To make dressing, place sugar, vinegar and black pepper to taste in a screwtop jar and shake well to combine. Pour dressing over tomato mixture and toss to combine. Cover and marinate, at room temperature, for 20 minutes before serving.*

Serves 4

ingredients

**4 tomatoes, thickly sliced
125g/4oz reduced-fat feta
cheese, chopped
¹/₂ red onion, sliced
3 tablespoons fresh basil leaves
<u>Balsamic dressing</u>
1 tablespoon brown sugar
¹/₄ cup/60ml/2fl oz balsamic vinegar
freshly ground black pepper**

salad
of roast tomatoes

Method:

1 Place tomatoes and garlic on a baking tray, sprinkle with black pepper to taste and oil and bake for 30 minutes or until tomatoes are soft and golden. Set aside to cool completely.
2 Arrange lettuce leaves, feta cheese, yellow or red capsicum (pepper), tomatoes and garlic attractively on serving plates.
3 To make dressing, place vinegar, tomato purée, Tabasco and black pepper to taste in a screwtop jar and shake well to combine. Drizzle dressing over salad and serve immediately.

Note: The sweet, rich flavour of roast tomatoes is a perfect partner for the creamy piquant feta cheese in this salad.

Serves 4

ingredients

6 plum (egg or Italian) tomatoes, halved
8 cloves garlic, peeled
freshly ground black pepper
2 tablespoons olive oil
315g/10oz assorted lettuce leaves
185g/6oz feta cheese, crumbled
1 yellow or red capsicum (pepper), sliced
Tangy dressing
3 tablespoons balsamic or red wine vinegar
3 tablespoons tomato purée
3 drops Tabasco sauce
freshly ground black pepper

Oven temperature 180°C, 350°F, Gas 4

oriental
coleslaw in curry

Method:

1 Place Chinese and red cabbages in a bowl and toss to combine, then arrange.

2 Place carrot, celery, spring onions, red capsicum (pepper), bean sprouts and mint and coriander leaves in a bowl and toss to combine. Arrange vegetable mixture on top of cabbage mixture.

3 To make dressing, place curry powder, sugar, yogurt, sour cream and lemon juice in a bowl and whisk to combine. Drizzle dressing over salad, then scatter with sesame seeds and serve with fried noodles.

Note: The thickness of the dressing will depend on the type of yogurt used, if it is too thick, whisk in a little water.

Serves 4

ingredients

¹/₄ **Chinese cabbage, finely shredded**
¹/₄ **red cabbage, finely shredded**
1 **carrot, cut into thin strips**
2 **stalks celery, cut into thin strips**
4 **spring onions, thinly sliced**
¹/₂ **red capsicum (pepper), cut into thin strips**
60g/2oz **bean sprouts**
¹/₂ **bunch fresh mint**
¹/₂ **bunch fresh coriander**
1 **tablespoon black sesame seeds, toasted**
60g/2oz **fried egg noodles**
<u>**Curry dressing**</u>
1 **teaspoon curry powder**
1 **teaspoon brown sugar**
1 **cup/200g/6¹/₂ oz natural yogurt**
2 **tablespoons sour cream**
1 **teaspoon lemon juice**

grilled prawn salad

seafood
salads

As a main meal or as a starter,

*a seafood salad is always welcome. In this
chapter you will find exciting recipes for
salads, such as Warm Seafood Salad or
Grilled Prawn Salad. Whichever one you
choose, you can be sure that it will not only
taste great but will be good for you as well.*

seafood
salads

marinated
citrus fish

Method:

1 Place fish in a glass bowl with peppercorns and orange rind.
2 To make marinade, combine oil, orange, grapefruit and lime juices, vinegar and ginger. Pour marinade over fish, cover and refrigerate overnight.
3 To serve, use a slotted spoon to remove fish to a bowl. Add lychees, orange and grapefruit segments to fish mixture. Toss lightly to combine. Arrange watercress on a plate and top with fish salad. Spoon over a little of the marinade.

Serves 4

ingredients

500g/1 lb white fish fillets, cut into strips
2 teaspoons pink peppercorns
2 teaspoons orange rind
440g/14oz canned lychees, drained
1 orange, peeled and segmented
1 grapefruit, peeled and segmented
1/2 bunch fresh watercress
Marinade
1 tablespoon grape seed oil
125mL/4fl oz orange juice
1 tablespoon grapefruit juice
1 tablespoon lime juice
1 tablespoon tarragon vinegar
1 teaspoon grated fresh ginger

grilled
prawn salad

Method:

1 Place prawns, chilli, soy sauce and honey in a bowl, toss to combine and marinate for 5 minutes.
2 Arrange witlof (chicory), radicchio, mangoes, mint and coriander (cilantro) on serving plates. Combine sugar and lime juice and drizzle over salad.
3 Heat a nonstick frying pan over a high heat, add prawns and stir-fry for 2 minutes or until cooked. Place prawns on top of salad, spoon over pan juices and serve immediately.

Serves 4

ingredients

16 uncooked prawns, shelled and deveined, tails left intact
1 fresh green chilli, seeded and shredded
1/4 cup/60ml/2fl oz reduced-salt soy sauce
1 tablespoon honey
1 witlof (chicory), leaves separated
1 radicchio, leaves separated
2 green (unripe) mangoes, thinly sliced
4 tablespoons fresh mint leaves
3 tablespoons fresh coriander (cilantro) leaves
1 tablespoon brown sugar
2 tablespoons lime juice

chickpea
and trout salad

Method:

1 Arrange endive and rocket on a serving platter. Top with chickpeas, goat's cheese, onion and trout. Sprinkle salad with basil and top with red capsicum (pepper).

2 To make dressing, place yoghurt, mint, cumin, honey and lime juice in a bowl and mix to combine. Drizzle dressing over salad and serve immediately.

Note: Chickpeas are slightly crunchy and lend a nutty flavour to salads like this as well as casseroles, soups and other savoury dishes. Dried chickpeas can be used rather than canned if you wish. To cook chickpeas, soak overnight in cold water. Drain. Place in a large saucepan, cover with cold water and bring to the boil over a medium heat. Reduce heat and simmer for 45-60 minutes or until chickpeas are tender. Drain and cool.

Serves 4

ingredients

1 bunch curly endive, leaves separated
1 bunch rocket
440g/14oz canned chickpeas, rinsed and drained
125g/4oz herbed goat's cheese, crumbled
1 red onion, sliced
250g/8oz smoked trout, skin and bones removed, flesh flaked
2 tablespoons chopped fresh basil
1 red capsicum (pepper), halved, roasted, skin removed and sliced
<u>Honey lime dressing</u>
1/2 cup/100g/3 1/2oz natural yoghurt
1 tablespoon chopped fresh mint
1 tablespoon ground cumin
1 tablespoon honey
1 tablespoon lime juice

seafood
salads

Method:

1 *Arrange salad leaves, teardrop tomatoes (if using) and cherry tomatoes, avocados, snow peas (mangetout) and asparagus on a large serving platter.*

2 *To make dressing, place vinegar, fish sauce, chilli sauce, basil, lemon juice and water in a small bowl and whisk to combine. Set aside.*

3 *Cut calamari (squid) tubes, lengthwise, and open out flat. Using a sharp knife, cut parallel lines down the length of the calamari (squid), taking care not to cut right through the flesh. Make more cuts in the opposite direction to form a diamond pattern. Cut each piece into 5 cm/2 in squares.*

4 *Melt butter in a large frying pan, add scallops and prawns and stir-fry for 3 minutes. Add calamari (squid) pieces and stir-fry for 1 minute longer. Arrange cooked seafood and smoked ocean trout or smoked salmon on salad and drizzle with dressing.*

Note: *This salad is great served warm, but also may be made ahead of time and served chilled. If serving chilled, prepare the salad, seafood and dressing and store separately in the refrigerator. Just prior to serving, assemble the salad as described in the recipe.*

Serves 8

warm
seafood salad

ingredients

500g/1 lb assorted salad leaves
250g/8oz yellow teardrop tomatoes (optional)
250g/8oz cherry tomatoes, halved
2 avocados, stoned, peeled and sliced
155g/5oz snow peas (mangetout), trimmed, blanched
250g/8oz asparagus spears, cut into 5cm/2in pieces, blanched
3 calamari (squid) tubes
30g/1oz butter
250g/8oz scallops
16 uncooked medium prawns, shelled and deveined, tails left intact
200g/6¹/₂oz thickly sliced smoked ocean trout or smoked salmon
<u>Oriental dressing</u>
1 tablespoon rice vinegar
1 tablespoon fish sauce
2 tablespoons sweet chilli sauce
1 tablespoon shredded fresh basil
1 tablespoon lemon juice
¹/₄ cup/60ml/2fl oz water

asparagus
and salmon salad

Method:

1 Boil, steam or microwave asparagus until tender. Drain, refresh under cold running water, drain again and chill. Arrange lettuce leaves, asparagus and salmon on serving plates.

2 To make sauce, place yogurt, lemon rind, lemon juice, dill and cumin in a small bowl and mix to combine.

3 Spoon sauce over salad. Sprinkle with black pepper, cover and chill until required.

Note: If fresh asparagus is unavailable, green beans or snow peas (mangetout) are good alternatives for this recipe.

ingredients

750g/1 ¹/₂ lb asparagus spears, trimmed
lettuce leaves of your choice
500g/1 lb smoked salmon slices
freshly ground black pepper
<u>**Lemon yoghurt sauce**</u>
1 cup/200g/6¹/₂oz natural
low-fat yoghurt
1 tablespoon finely grated lemon rind
1 tablespoon lemon juice
1 tablespoon chopped fresh dill
1 teaspoon ground cumin

scallops
and wilted spinach

Method:

1 Preheat barbecue to a medium heat.
2 To make salad, blanch spinach leaves in boiling water for 10 seconds. Drain spinach, refresh under cold running water, drain again and place in a bowl.
3 Place sesame seeds, soy sauce, lemon juice and sesame oil in a bowl and mix to combine. Spoon dressing over spinach and toss to combine. Divide salad between serving plates.
4 Place scallops in bowl, drizzle with a little vegetable oil and season to taste with black pepper. Sear scallops on barbecue plate (griddle) for 45-60 seconds or until golden and flesh is opaque. Place scallops on top of each salad and serve immediately.
Note: Alternatively the scallops can be seared in a hot frying pan.
Serves 6

ingredients

18 scallops
vegetable oil
crushed black peppercorns
Wilted spinach salad
185g/6oz baby English spinach leaves
2 teaspoons sesame seeds
2 tablespoons soy sauce
1 tablespoon lemon juice
2 teaspoons sesame oil

34

salad
of lobster with raspberries

Method:

1 Cut lobster tails into 1cm medallions and set aside.
2 Arrange radicchio, mignonette, sprouts or watercress, lobster, orange segments and strawberries attractively on a serving platter and refrigerate until required.
3 To make dressing, place raspberries in a food processor or blender and process until pureed. Push through a sieve to remove seeds. Combine raspberry puree with vinegar, oil, mint and sugar. Mix well to combine, pour over salad and serve immediately.

Note: Lobster would have to be the undisputed king of shellfish. In this recipe, it is taken to new heights with the addition of a raspberry dressing.

Serves 4

ingredients

2 lobster tails, cooked and shells removed
1 small radicchio, leaves separated
1 small mignonette lettuce,
leaves separated
100g/3oz snow pea sprouts or watercress
1 orange, segmented
250g/8oz strawberries, halved
<u>**Dressing**</u>
125g/4oz fresh or frozen raspberries
2 tablespoons raspberry vinegar
2 tablespoons vegetable oil
1 teaspoon finely chopped fresh mint
1 tablespoon sugar

thai
squid salad

Method:

1 Using a sharp knife, make a single cut down the length of each squid (calamari) tube and open out. Cut parallel lines down the length of the squid (calamari), taking care not to cut right the way through the flesh. Make more cuts in the opposite direction to form a diamond pattern.

2 Heat a nonstick char-grill or frying pan over a high heat, add squid (calamari) and cook for 1-2 minutes each side or until tender. Remove from pan and cut into thin strips.

3 Place squid (calamari), beans, tomatoes, pawpaw, spring onions, mint, coriander and chilli in a serving bowl.

4 To make dressing, place sugar, lime juice and fish sauce in a screwtop jar and shake well. Drizzle over salad and toss to combine. Cover and stand for 20 minutes before serving.

Serving suggestion: Soy Rice Noodles - boil 375g/12oz fresh rice noodles, drain and sprinkle with a little reduced-salt soy sauce. Scatter with a few toasted sesame seeds and toss to combine.

ingredients

3 squid (calamari) tubes, cleaned
185g/6oz green beans, sliced lengthwise
2 tomatoes, cut into wedges
1 small green pawpaw, peeled, seeded and shredded
4 spring onions, sliced
30g/1oz fresh mint leaves
30g/1oz fresh coriander (cilantro) leaves
1 fresh red chilli, chopped
<u>**Lime dressing**</u>
2 teaspoons brown sugar
3 tablespoons lime juice
1 tablespoon fish sauce

Serves 4

tuna
and lemon pasta

Method:

1 Cook fettuccine in boiling water in a large saucepan following packet directions. Drain and return pasta to saucepan.
2 Place pan over a low heat, add tuna, rocket, cheese, dill, lemon juice and black pepper to taste and toss to combine. Serve immediately.

Serves 4

ingredients

500g/1 lb fettuccine
440g/14oz canned tuna in spring water, drained and flaked
185g/6oz rocket leaves, roughly chopped
155g/5oz reduced-fat feta cheese, chopped
1 tablespoon chopped fresh dill
¼ cup/60ml/2fl oz lemon juice
freshly ground black pepper

tarragon
seafood salad

Method:

1 Place tarragon, lime juice, lime rind, chilli, oil and black pepper to taste in a bowl and mix to combine. Add lobster, toss to coat and set aside to marinate for 15 minutes.

2 Arrange snow pea sprouts or watercress, cucumber, carrot and red capsicum (pepper) on a large serving platter and set aside.

3 Heat a char-grill or frying pan over a high heat, add lobster mixture and cook, turning frequently, for 2 minutes or until lobster is tender. Arrange lobster over salad, spoon over pan juices and serve immediately.

Note: To make cucumber and carrot ribbons, use a vegetable peeler to remove strips lengthwise from the cucumber or carrot. This salad is also delicious made using prawns instead of lobster. If using prawns, shell and devein them before marinating.

Serves 4

ingredients

4 tablespoons chopped fresh tarragon
2 tablespoons lime juice
3 teaspoons grated lime rind
1 fresh red chilli, chopped
2 teaspoons olive oil
freshly ground black pepper
500g/1 lb uncooked lobster tail, flesh removed from shell and cut into large pieces or 500g/1 lb firm white fish fillets, cut into large pieces
250g/8oz snow pea sprouts or watercress
1 cucumber, sliced into ribbons
2 carrots, sliced into ribbons
1 red capsicum (pepper), cut into thin strips

Method:

1 To make dressing, place mayonnaise, olive oil, vinegar and mustard in a bowl, mix to combine and set aside.

2 Heat sesame oil in a frying pan over a high heat, add garlic and scallops and cook, stirring, for 1 minute or until scallops just turn opaque. Remove scallop mixture from pan and set aside. Add bacon to pan and cook, stirring, for 4 minutes or until crisp. Remove bacon from pan and drain on absorbent kitchen paper.

3 Place lettuce leaves in a large salad bowl, add dressing and toss to coat. Add bacon, croûtons and shavings of Parmesan cheese and toss to combine. Spoon scallop mixture over salad and serve.

seared
scallop salad

ingredients

2 teaspoons sesame oil
2 cloves garlic, crushed
375g/12oz scallops, cleaned
4 rashers bacon, chopped
1 cos lettuce, leaves separated
60g/2oz croûtons
fresh Parmesan cheese
Mustard dressing
3 tablespoons mayonnaise
1 tablespoon olive oil
1 tablespoon vinegar
2 teaspoons Dijon mustard

chicken caesar salad

meat salads

Succulent strips or slices of meat

tossed or drizzled with a tangy dressing are the basis of these meat salads. Perfect as light meals, these salads are substantial enough to satisfy the hungriest diners.

green
mango salad

Method:

1 Arrange lettuce, cucumber, mangoes, chicken, mint and coriander attractively on a serving platter.
2 To make dressing, place chillies, sugar, lime juice and fish sauce in a bowl and mix to combine. Drizzle dressing over salad and serve.
Note: *Palm sugar is a rich, aromatic sugar extracted from the sap of various palms. The palm sugar used in Thailand is lighter and more refined than that used in other parts of Asia. Palm sugar is available from Oriental food shops. If green (unripe) mangoes are unavailable you might like to make this salad using tart green apples instead.*

Serves 4

ingredients

125g/4oz mixed lettuce leaves
1 cucumber, thinly sliced
2 green (unripe) mangoes, peeled and thinly sliced
250g/8oz cooked chicken, shredded
4 tablespoons fresh mint leaves
4 tablespoons fresh coriander leaves
<u>**Chilli and lime dressing**</u>
2 fresh red chillies, chopped
2 tablespoons palm or brown sugar
3 tablespoons lime juice
2 teaspoons Thai fish sauce (nam pla)

chicken
caesar salad

Photograph page 44

Method:

1 Preheat barbecue to a medium heat.
2 To make croûtons, place bread cubes in a baking dish, drizzle with oil and toss to coat. Bake for 15 minutes or until bread is crisp and golden. Cool.
3 Place chicken and bacon on oiled barbecue and cook for 2-3 minutes each side or until chicken is tender and bacon is crisp. Cool, then cut chicken into slices and chop bacon.
4 Arrange lettuce leaves, tomatoes, chicken and bacon in a bowl.
5 To make dressing, place sour cream, mayonnaise, mustard, anchovies and water in a food processor or blender and process until smooth. Just prior to serving, drizzle dressing over salad, then scatter with croûtons and parmesan cheese shavings.
Note: *To make the bread cubes for the croûtons, take an unsliced loaf of stale bread and cut off all the crusts to make an evenly shaped rectangular loaf. Cut bread loaf into 5mm/¹/₄ in thick slices. Cut each bread slice into 5mm/¹/₄ in thick strips, then cut in the opposite direction at 5mm/¹/₄ in intervals to make 5 mm/1/4 in square bread cubes. Using a whole loaf of bread will make more croûtons than you require for this recipe, however, leftover croûtons will keep in an airtight container for several weeks.*

ingredients

2 boneless chicken breast fillets
4 rashers bacon
1 cos lettuce, leaves separated
250g/8oz cherry tomatoes, halved
125g/4oz parmesan cheese shavings
<u>**Crispy croutons**</u>
250g/8oz bread cubes
2 tablespoons olive oil
<u>**Creamy mustard dressing**</u>
¹/₂ cup/125g/4oz sour cream
¹/₂ cup/125ml/4fl oz mayonnaise
2 tablespoons wholegrain mustard
3 anchovy fillets, chopped
¹/₄ cup/60ml/2fl oz water

Serves 8

Oven temperature 200°C, 400°F, Gas 6

warm
beef and potato salad

Method:

1 Roll beef in black peppercorns. Heat 1 tablespoon oil in a frying pan over a medium heat, add beef and cook for 10-15 minutes, turning frequently, until well browned on all sides, continue cooking until beef is cooked to your liking. Remove beef from pan, cover, set aside and keep warm.

2 Wipe pan clean with absorbent kitchen paper. Add 5cm/2in of oil and heat until a cube of bread dropped in browns in 50 seconds. Cook potato slices and sweet potato slices in batches for 3-5 minutes or until golden and crisp. Remove from pan, drain on absorbent kitchen paper and sprinkle with salt.

3 To serve, slice beef thinly. Divide potato crisps and lettuce leaves between serving plates. Place beef slices on top of lettuce, sprinkle with vinegar and serve immediately.
Note: When the beef is browned it will be rare to medium. If this is how you like your meat, remove it from the pan at this stage.

ingredients

500g/1 lb fillet of beef in one piece
2 tablespoons crushed black
peppercorns
vegetable oil
4 potatoes, very thinly sliced
1 large orange sweet potato,
very thinly sliced
salt
assorted lettuce leaves
balsamic or red wine vinegar

To test the degree of doneness of the meat, press it with a pair of blunt tongs. Rare meat will feel springy to the touch, medium meat slightly springy and well-done meat will feel firm.
Serves 4

chicken
and nectarine salad

Method:

1 Arrange lettuce leaves, watercress, chicken, red pepper, nectarines and celery in a salad bowl or on a large serving platter.

2 To make dressing, place black peppercorns, oil and vinegar in a screwtop jar and shake well to combine. Spoon dressing over salad and serve immediately.

Note: This spectacular salad is ideal for a simple summer luncheon.

Serves 4

ingredients

1 lettuce of your choice, leaves separated
1 bunch/250g/8oz watercress, broken into sprigs
500g/1 lb cooked chicken, chopped
1 red capsicum (pepper), sliced
4 nectarines, sliced
2 stalks celery, sliced
Black pepper dressing
3 teaspoons crushed black peppercorns
1 tablespoon olive oil
2 tablespoons red wine vinegar

cellophane
noodle salad

Method:

1 Place noodles in a bowl and pour over boiling water to cover. Stand for 10 minutes, then drain well.

2 Heat oil in a frying pan over a high heat, add garlic and ginger and stir-fry for 1 minute. Add pork and stir-fry for 5 minutes or until pork is browned and cooked through.

3 Arrange mint, coriander, lettuce, shallots, chilli and noodles on a serving platter. Top with pork mixture, then drizzle with lemon juice and soy sauce.

Note: *Cellophane noodles, also known as glass noodles, bean thread noodles or vermicelli, are made from mung bean flour and are either very thin vermicelli-style noodles or flatter fettuccine-style noodles. In the dried state they are very tough and difficult to break. For ease of use it is best to buy a brand which packages them as bundles.*

Serves 4

ingredients

155g/5oz cellophane noodles
2 teaspoons sesame oil
2 cloves garlic, crushed
1 tablespoon finely grated fresh ginger
500g/1 lb pork mince
15g/½oz mint leaves
15g/½oz coriander (cilantro) leaves
8 lettuce leaves
5 red or golden shallots, chopped
1 fresh red chilli, sliced
2 tablespoons lemon juice
1 tablespoon light soy sauce

Oven temperature 180°C

marsala
quail salad

ingredients

Method:
1 Place quails on a rack in a baking pan and bake for 20 minutes. Cool slightly, then break into serving-size portions.
2 Melt butter in a saucepan. Add cream and Marsala, bring to the boil, then reduce heat and simmer for 5 minutes. Add quail and cook for 5 minutes longer. Set aside to cool.
3 To make sauce, combine cream, mayonnaise and Marsala and beat well to combine.
4 Arrange endive, witloof, radicchio, watercress and pear in a serving bowl. Top with quail, sprinkle with pecans and drizzle sauce over. Serve immediately.

Note: In this salad the quail and marsala, with their distinctive flavours, mingle deliciously with the salad leaves. An elegant dish that can be served as a luncheon dish or starter.

Serves 6

6 quails
30g/1 oz butter
¹/₂ cup/125ml/4fl oz cream
³/₄ cup/185ml/6fl oz dry Marsala
1 curly endive, leaves separated
1 witloof, leaves separated
1 radicchio, leaves separated
1 bunch/200g/7oz watercress
1 pear, peeled, cored and sliced
45g/1¹/₂oz pecans
Marsala sauce
2 tablespoons mayonnaise
2 teaspoons dry Marsala
1 tablespoon cream

smoked
chicken in ginger dressing

ingredients

Method:

1 Place chicken, shallots, red capsicum (pepper), chilli, coriander (cilantro) and mint in a serving bowl. Season to taste with black pepper.

2 To make dressing, place oil, vinegar, orange juice, mustard, sugar and ginger in a screwtop jar and shake well to combine. Pour over chicken mixture and toss to combine. Cover and refrigerate.

Note: A pretty salad with a fresh taste that is easy to make and travels well. Put the salad in the serving bowl to marinate on the way to your picnic.

Serves 6

1 smoked chicken, 1-1½kg, meat removed and broken into bite-size pieces
4 green shallots, finely chopped
1 small red capsicum (pepper), finely sliced
1 small red chilli, seeded and finely sliced
1 tablespoon chopped fresh coriander (cilantro)
1 tablespoon chopped fresh mint
freshly ground black pepper
Orange and ginger dressing
3 tablespoons olive oil
2 tablespoons white wine vinegar
2 tablespoons freshly squeezed orange juice
1 teaspoon wholegrain mustard
1 teaspoon brown sugar
1 teaspoon finely grated fresh ginger

italian
chicken salad

Method:

1 *Heat a nonstick char-grill or frying pan over a high heat. Lightly spray chicken with olive oil, add to pan and cook for 2-3 minutes each side or until tender. Remove from pan and set aside to cool.*

2 *To make dressing, place prunes, oregano, lemon rind, sugar and vinegar in a saucepan over a low heat, bring to simmering and simmer for 5 minutes.*

3 *To assemble salad, cut chicken breasts into thin slices. Arrange spinach, beans, onion, chicken and capers attractively on serving plates. Drizzle a little warm dressing over the salad and serve immediately. Serve any remaining dressing separately.*

Serves 4

ingredients

**13 boneless chicken breast fillets,
all visible fat and skin removed
olive oil spray
125g/4oz baby English spinach leaves
125g/4oz green beans, blanched
1 red onion, thinly sliced
2 tablespoons small capers, drained
<u>Vinegar and Prune Dressing</u>
8 pitted prunes
1 tablespoon fresh oregano leaves
shredded rind of 1 lemon
1 teaspoon sugar
1/2 cup/125ml/4fl oz red wine vinegar**

warm
pork and mint salad

Method:

1 Heat a nonstick frying pan or wok over a medium heat, add shallots, ginger and chilli and cook, stirring, for 3 minutes.

2 Add pork and stir-fry for 3-4 minutes or until brown. Stir in mint, sugar, soy sauce, lime juice and fish sauce and stir-fry for 4 minutes or until pork is cooked.

3 Arrange lettuce leaves, cucumber and snow pea (mangetout) sprouts or watercress on a serving platter, top with pork mixture and serve immediately.

Note: For an easy dessert, serve Chilled Nashis with Lime - cut chilled nashis into thin slices, sprinkle with fresh lime juice and toss. Nashis are at their best during the winter months and this easy dessert is a refreshing and healthy way to end any meal. If Vietnamese mint is unavailable use ordinary mint instead.

Serves 4

ingredients

6 shallots, chopped
2 tablespoons shredded fresh ginger
1 fresh red chilli, chopped
500g/1 lb lean minced pork
3 tablespoons shredded Vietnamese mint
1 tablespoon brown sugar
1/4 cup/60ml/2fl oz reduced-salt soy sauce
2 tablespoons lime juice
2 teaspoons Thai fish sauce
250g/8oz assorted lettuce leaves
1 cucumber, sliced
60g/2oz snow pea (mangetout)
sprouts or watercress

chicken
and couscous salad

Method:
1 *Place couscous in a bowl, pour over boiling water and stock, cover and stand for 5 minutes or until water is absorbed. Toss with a fork to separate grains.*
2 *Arrange lettuce, couscous, chicken, tomatoes, cucumber, coriander and snow pea (mangetout) sprouts or watercress on a serving platter.*
3 *To make dressing, place mint, cumin, chilli powder and yoghurt in a bowl and whisk to combine. Drizzle a little dressing over salad and serve remaining dressing separately.*

Serves 4

ingredients

1 cup/185g/6oz couscous
¹/₂ cup/125ml/4fl oz boiling water
¹/₂ cup/125ml/4fl oz boiling chicken stock
1 cos lettuce, leaves separated
250g/8oz cooked chicken breast fillets, cut into thick slices
2 tomatoes, chopped
1 cucumber, chopped
3 tablespoons fresh coriander (cilantro) leaves
60g/2oz snow pea (mangetout) sprouts or watercress
<u>Yoghurt dressing</u>
2 tablespoons chopped fresh mint
1 teaspoon ground cumin
¹/₂ teaspoon chilli powder
1 cup/200g/6¹/₂oz low-fat yoghurt

thai
beef salad

Method:

1 Heat a frying or char-grill pan over a high heat until hot, add beef and cook for 1-2 minutes each side or until cooked to your liking. Set aside to cool.

2 Arrange lettuce, tomatoes, cucumbers, onions and mint attractively on a serving platter.

3 To make dressing, place lemon grass or rind, coriander (cilanto), sugar, lime juice and soy, chilli and fish sauces in a bowl and mix to combine.

4 Slice beef thinly and arrange on salad, then drizzle with dressing and serve.

Note: When making a Thai salad, presentation is all important and a salad can be a spectacular centrepiece for any table. Traditionally Thai salads are served on flat plates - not in bowls - which means the full effect of the arrangement of ingredients can be appreciated.

Serves 4

ingredients

500g/1 lb rump or topside steak
185g/6 oz mixed lettuce leaves
185g/6oz cherry tomatoes, halved
2 cucumbers, peeled and chopped
2 red onions, sliced
3 tablespoons fresh mint leaves
<u>**Lime and Coriander dressing**</u>
1 stalk fresh lemon grass, chopped or
1 teaspoon finely grated lemon rind
3 tablespoons fresh coriander
(cilanto) leaves
1 tablespoon brown sugar
2 tablespoons lime juice
3 tablespoons light soy sauce
2 tablespoons sweet chilli sauce
2 teaspoons Thai fish sauce (nam pla)

nutty
pork ravioli salad

Method:

1 *To make filling, heat oil in a nonstick frying pan over a medium heat, add garlic and cook, stirring, for 2 minutes. Add pork and cook, stirring, for 5 minutes. Remove pan from heat, stir in peanut butter, chilli sauce, mint and soy sauce. Place a tablespoon of filling in the centre of each wrapper, brush edges with a little water, then top with a second wrapper and press edges to seal.*

2 *Place in a steamer set over a saucepan of boiling water, cover and steam in batches for 5 minutes or until ravioli is tender. Set aside and keep warm.*

3 *To make dressing, combine water, lime juice, chilli sauce, fish sauce and coriander (cilantro) in a bowl. Arrange lettuce leaves on a serving platter, top with warm ravioli and spoon over dressing.*

32 spring roll or wonton wrappers, each 7¹/₂cm/3in square
assorted lettuce leaves
<u>Chilli pork filling</u>
I tablespoon sesame oil
I clove garlic, finely chopped
250g/8oz lean pork mince
I tablespoon crunchy peanut butter
I tablespoon sweet chilli sauce
I tablespoon chopped fresh mint
2 teaspoons reduced-salt soy sauce
<u>Chilli dressing</u>
¹/₄ cup/60ml/2fl oz warm water
2 tablespoons lime juice
I tablespoon sweet chilli sauce
I tablespoon fish sauce
3 tablespoons chopped fresh coriander (cilantro)

thai
lamb salad

Method:

1 *To make dressing, place coriander (cilantro), sugar, soy and chilli sauces, lime juice and fish sauce in a bowl and mix to combine. Set aside.*

2 *Arrange lettuce leaves and cucumber on a serving platter and set aside.*

3 *Heat oil in a wok over a high heat, add lamb and stir-fry for 2 minutes or until brown. Place lamb on top of lettuce leaves, drizzle with dressing and serve immediately.*

Note: *This salad is also delicious made with pork fillet. Use a vegetable peeler to make long thin slices of cucumber - simply peel off lengthwise strips.*

Serves 4

250g/8oz assorted lettuce leaves
I cucumber, sliced lengthwise into thin strips
2 teaspoons vegetable oil
500g/1 lb lamb fillets, trimmed of all visible fat, thinly sliced
<u>Coriander and Chilli Dressing</u>
2 tablespoons chopped fresh coriander (cilantro)
I tablespoon brown sugar
¹/₄ cup/60ml/2fl oz soy sauce
2 tablespoons sweet chilli sauce
2 tablespoons lime juice
2 teaspoons fish sauce

new
mexico chicken salad

Method:

1 Arrange rocket, flowers and radicchio attractively on serving plates. Top with grapefruit and chicken.

2 To make dressing, place pine nuts, bay leaves, chillies, sugar, vinegar and oil in a bowl and whisk to combine. Just prior to serving, drizzle dressing over salad.

Note: Edible flowers you might like to choose from include nasturtiums, scented geraniums, roses, marigolds, violets, zucchini (courgette) flowers and the flowers of most herbs such as chives, rocket, borage, dill, rosemary, lavender and basil. Look out for mixed packs of edible flowers in greengrocers and specialty food shops.

Serves 4

ingredients

**1 bunch young rocket
edible flowers of your choice
6 radicchio leaves, shredded
1 grapefruit, peeled, all white pith
removed, segmented
2 smoked chicken breasts, sliced**
<u>**Pine nut and chilli dressing**</u>
**4 tablespoons pine nuts, toasted
6 bay leaves
2 fresh red chillies, finely chopped
2 tablespoons sugar
1/3 cup/90ml/3fl oz red wine vinegar
1/4 cup/60ml/2fl oz olive oil**

chicken
and curry salad

Method:

1 Heat oil in a wok over a medium heat, add garlic, ginger, chillies and onion and stir-fry for 3 minutes or until onion is golden. Add curry paste and stir-fry for 3 minutes longer or until fragrant.

2 Stir chicken, fish sauce and sugar into pan and cook, stirring frequently, for 10 minutes or until chicken is tender. Remove pan from heat and set aside to cool slightly. Add mint and coriander and toss to combine.

3 To serve, line a large platter with cabbage, then top with spring onions, cucumbers, bean sprouts, red capsicum (pepper) and chicken mixture.

Serves 4

ingredients

1 tablespoon sesame oil
1 clove garlic, crushed
1 tablespoon finely grated fresh ginger
2 small fresh red chillies, finely chopped
1 onion, cut in wedges
1 tablespoon Thai Green Curry Paste
500g/1 lb boneless chicken breast fillets, thinly sliced
1 tablespoon Thai fish sauce (nam pla)
1 tablespoon sugar
2 tablespoons chopped fresh mint
1 tablespoon chopped fresh coriander (cilantro)
1 Chinese cabbage, sliced
3 spring onions, sliced
2 cucumbers, sliced
125g/4oz bean sprouts
1 red capsicum (pepper), thinly sliced

spiced
grilled beef

Method:

1 Place onion, garlic, coriander roots, peppercorns, soy sauce, lime juice and fish sauce in a food processor and process to make a paste. Coat beef with spice mixture and cook over a medium charcoal or gas barbecue, turning occasionally, for 15 minutes or until beef is cooked to medium doneness. Alternatively, bake beef in oven for 30-45 minutes or until cooked to medium .

2 Arrange lettuce, tomatoes and cucumber on a serving plate. Slice beef thinly and arrange over lettuce. Serve with lime wedges.

Serves 4

ingredients

1 red onion, chopped
4 cloves garlic, crushed
2 fresh coriander (cilantro) roots
1 teaspoon crushed black peppercorns
2 tablespoons light soy sauce
2 teaspoons lime juice
2 teaspoons Thai fish sauce (nam pla)
500g/1 lb rib-eye (scotch fillet) of beef,
in one piece
6 lettuce leaves
185g/6oz cherry tomatoes, halved
1 cucumber, cut into strips
lime wedges

mexican corn and bean salad

bean, pasta & rice salads

Salads made with beans, pasta

and rice make satisfying and substantial meals. Next time you are looking for a warm-weather main dish, why not try a Warm Rice or Marinated Bean Salad.

pasta
shell salad

ingredients

75g/2¹/₂oz pasta shells, cooked
¹/₂ avocado, peeled and chopped
3 tablespoons drained, canned
sweet corn kernels
¹/₂ tomato, chopped
2 tablespoons mayonnaise
2 tablespoons natural yoghurt

Method:

1 *Place pasta, avocado, sweet corn and tomato in a bowl and toss to combine. Mix together mayonnaise and yoghurt, drizzle over salad and toss to combine.*

Serves 2

mexican
corn bean salad

Photograph page 60
ingredients

375g/1 oz canned sweet corn kernels, drained
375g/12oz canned red kidney beans,
rinsed and drained
90g/3oz green beans, blanched
and cut into 5cm/2in pieces
1 large red capsicum (pepper), diced
1 large green capsicum (pepper), diced
3 tomatoes, chopped
2 avocados, chopped
<u>Chilli and herb dressing</u>
1 red onion, chopped
3 small fresh green chillies,
finely chopped
2 cloves garlic, crushed
3 tablespoons chopped fresh coriander
(cilantro)
2 teaspoons ground cumin
¹/₃ cup/90ml/3fl oz balsamic vinegar
¹/₄ cup/60ml/2fl oz olive oil

Method:

1 *Place sweet corn, red kidney and green beans, red and green capsicum(peppers), tomatoes and avocados in a salad bowl and toss to combine.*

2 *To make dressing, place onion, chillies, garlic, coriander, cumin, vinegar and oil in a bowl and whisk to combine.*

3 *Drizzle dressing over salad and toss to combine. Cover and refrigerate for 1 hour before serving.*

Note: *To blanch green beans, bring a large saucepan of water to the boil, add beans and cook until they are bright green. Remove immediately and refresh under cold running water. For a delicious light meal serve this salad on fried tortillas or wrapped in pitta bread.*

Serves 6

minestrone

Method:

1 Cook pasta in boiling water in a large saucepan following packet directions. Drain, rinse under cold running water and set aside to cool completely.

2 Place chickpeas, carrots, zucchini (courgettes), celery, red capsicum (pepper), beans, tomatoes and pasta in a bowl and toss to combine.

3 Arrange lettuce on a serving platter and top with pasta mixture.

4 To make dressing, place pesto, yoghurt and mayonnaise in a bowl and mix to combine. Drizzle over salad and serve.

Note: This dish makes the most of all the flavours ordinarily found in minestrone soup and serves them up as a salad! If plum (egg or Italian) tomatoes are not available, substitute ordinary tomatoes.

Serves 4

ingredients

250g/8oz pasta shells
440g/14oz canned chickpeas, rinsed and drained
2 carrots, diced
2 zucchini (courgettes), diced
2 stalks celery, diced
1 red capsicum (pepper), diced
155g/5oz green beans, blanched
3 plum (egg or Italian) tomatoes, cut into wedges
250g/8oz mixed lettuce leaves
Pesto dressing
125g/4oz ready-made pesto
1/2 cup/100g/3 1/2oz natural yoghurt
2 tablespoons mayonnaise

spicy
wild rice salad

Method:

1 Cook rice in boiling water following packet directions or until tender. Drain well and set aside to cool.

2 Heat oil in a nonstick frying pan over a medium heat, add onions, cumin, cinnamon, cloves and ginger and cook, stirring, for 10 minutes or until onions are soft and slightly caramelised. Add carrots and cook until tender. Stir in honey, then remove from heat and cool slightly.

3 Place rice, carrot mixture, oranges, pistachios, raisins, almonds, spring onions and dill in a bowl and toss to combine.

4 To make dressing, place mustard, oil, orange juice and vinegar in a bowl and whisk to combine. Pour dressing over salad and toss.

Note: If wild rice blend is unavailable use ³/₄ cup/170g/5¹/₂oz brown rice and ¹/₄ cup/60g/2oz wild rice. The two varieties of rice can be cooked together.

Serves 4

ingredients

2 cups/440g/14oz wild rice blend
(brown and wild rice mix)
2 tablespoons vegetable oil
2 onions, cut into thin wedges
1 teaspoon ground cumin
¹/₂ teaspoon ground cinnamon
¹/₄ teaspoon ground cloves
¹/₄ teaspoon ground ginger
2 carrots, thinly sliced
1 teaspoon honey
2 oranges, segmented
90g/3oz pistachios, toasted and
roughly chopped
90g/3oz raisins
60g/2oz flaked almonds, toasted
3 spring onions, sliced
3 tablespoons chopped fresh dill

Orange mustard dressing
1 teaspoon Dijon mustard
¹/₂ cup/125ml/4fl oz olive oil
¹/₄ cup/60ml/2fl oz orange juice
1 tablespoon red wine vinegar

pasta
and asparagus salad

Method:

1 Cook pasta in boiling water in a large saucepan following packet directions. Drain, rinse under cold running water, drain again and set aside.
2 Boil, steam or microwave asparagus until tender. Add asparagus and watercress to pasta and toss to combine.
3 Place butter and rosemary in a small saucepan and cook over a low heat until butter is golden. Divide pasta between serving bowls, then drizzle with rosemary-flavoured butter and top with black pepper and Parmesan cheese to taste. Serve with lime wedges.

Note: Chilli pasta is available from delicatessens and specialty food stores. If unavailable use ordinary pasta and add some chopped fresh chilli to the butter and rosemary mixture.

Serves 4

ingredients

500g/1 lb chilli linguine
250g/8oz asparagus, cut in half
155g/5oz watercress, broken into sprigs
60g/2oz butter
2 tablespoons chopped fresh rosemary
freshly ground black pepper
fresh Parmesan cheese shavings
lime wedges

bean
and broccoli salad

Method:

1 Boil, steam or microwave broccoli and beans, separately, until they just change colour. Drain and refresh under cold running water. Place in a bowl.

2 To make dressing, place pine nuts, basil, mint, lemon juice, oil and black pepper to taste in a bowl and mix to combine. Spoon dressing over vegetables and toss to combine.

Note: For a more colourful salad, use a combination of green and butter beans instead of just green.

Serves 8

ingredients

1kg/2 lb broccoli, broken into florets
155g/5oz green beans
Fresh herb dressing
60g/2oz pine nuts,
toasted and roughly chopped
2 tablespoons chopped fresh basil
1 tablespoon choppped fresh mint
1/3 cup/90ml/3fl oz lemon juice
1 tablespoon olive oil
freshly ground black pepper

---

beetroot
pasta salad

Method:

1 Cook beetroot in boiling water for 10-15 minutes or until tender. Drain and set aside to cool. Discard cooking water.

2 Cook pasta in clean boiling water in pan following packet directions. Drain, rinse under cold running water and set aside to cool completely.

3 Arrange lettuce leaves in a salad bowl, top with pasta, beetroot, carrots, zucchini (courgettes) and red capsicum (pepper).

4 To make dressing, place sesame seeds, oil, soy sauce and chilli sauce in a screwtop jar and shake well to combine. Spoon dressing over salad, cover and refrigerate until ready to serve.

Note: For an even quicker version of this dish canned baby beetroot could be used.

Serves 4

ingredients

Beetroot pasta salad
8 small beetroot, peeled and halved
375g/12oz fettuccine
250g/8oz assorted lettuce leaves
2 carrots, cut into thin strips
2 zucchini (courgettes), chopped
1 red capsicum (pepper), sliced
Sesame dressing
1 tablespoon sesame seeds
2 teaspoons sesame oil
2 tablespoons sweet soy sauce
2 tablespoons sweet chilli sauce

Oven temperature 180°C, 350°F, Gas 4

pasta
salad with roasted garlic

Method:

1 Place unpeeled garlic cloves on a lightly greased baking tray and bake for 10-12 minutes or until soft and golden. Peel garlic and set aside.

2 Cook bacon in a frying pan over a medium heat for 4-5 minutes or until crisp. Drain on absorbent kitchen paper.

3 Melt butter in a clean frying pan, add breadcrumbs, herbs and black pepper to taste and cook, stirring for 4-5 minutes or until breadcrumbs are golden.

4 Cook pasta in boiling water in a large saucepan following packet directions. Drain well and place in a warm serving bowl. Add garlic, bacon and breadcrumb mixture, toss and serve immediately.

Note: The garlic can be roasted and the bacon and breadcrumb mixture cooked several hours in advance, leaving just the cooking of the pasta and the final assembly of the salad to do at the last minute.

Serves 8

ingredients

20 cloves unpeeled garlic
8 rashers bacon, chopped
30g/1oz butter
2 cups/125g/4oz breadcrumbs,
made from stale bread
4 tablespoons chopped fresh mixed
herb leaves
freshly ground black pepper
750g/1 1/2 lb spinach, tomato or plain
linguine

drunken summer fruits

fruit
salads

A fruit salad makes a healthy,

*refreshing and light dessert that few people
can resist. The ways in which you can present
your fruit are almost endless. This chapter
presents a selection of fruit salads that you
will be proud to serve with any meal.*

orange
salad

ingredients

4 oranges
1/4 cup/60g/2oz sugar
1 cinnamon stick
3/4 cup/185ml/6fl oz water
1 teaspoon lemon juice
4 tablespoons reduced-fat
honey-flavoured yoghurt

Method:

1 *Thinly peel the rind from 1 orange. Ensure all the white pith is removed, cut rind into thin strips and set aside. Peel remaining oranges, remove all the white pith, and slice all oranges crossways into 1 cm/¹/₂ in thick slices. Place in a heatproof bowl and set aside.*

2 *Place reserved orange rind, sugar, cinnamon stick, water and lemon juice in saucepan over a medium heat, bring to simmering and simmer for 3 minutes. Remove from heat, cool slightly and pour over oranges. Cover and chill for at least 2 hours or until ready to serve. Serve with yoghurt.*

Note: *When blood oranges are in season they make a spectacular alternative to ordinary oranges in this simple dessert salad. Blood oranges are in season during winter months, however their season is short and they are not always easy to find.*

Serves 4

drunken
summer fruits

Photograph page 68

ingredients

375g/12oz mixed berries, such as
raspberries, blueberries and
strawberries
2 white peaches, quartered
2 nectarines, quartered
3/4 cup/185ml/6fl oz dessert wine
2 tablespoons lime juice
thick cream

Method:

1 *Place berries, peaches and nectarines in a bowl. Pour wine and lime juice over fruit and toss gently to combine. Cover and chill for 20-30 minutes. Serve in deep bowls with some of the marinade and a spoonful of thick cream.*

Note: *When available, fresh apricots are a tasty addition to this summer dessert.*

Serves 4-6

apple
strawberry and pecan salad

Method:

1 Combine apples, celery, strawberries, sultanas and pecans in a bowl.
2 To make dressing, blend together mint, yoghurt and lemon juice. Toss with apple mixture and refrigerate until required.
   Note: A variation on the traditional Waldorf salad, with half the fat and no cholesterol.

Serves 4

ingredients

2 red apples, chopped
2 stalks celery, sliced
185g/6oz strawberries, halved
3 tablespoons sultanas
60g/2oz chopped pecans
<u>Dressing</u>
2 teaspoons finely chopped
fresh mint leaves
3 tablespoons low-fat natural yoghurt
2 tablespoons lemon juice

berries
and passion fruit salad

Method:

1 *To make vinaigrette, place passion fruit pulp, vinegar, sugar, mustard and black pepper to taste in a screwtop jar and shake well to combine.*

2 *Arrange watercress, lettuce leaves, blueberries, tomatoes and cucumber on a serving platter. Spoon vinaigrette over salad and serve immediately.*

Note: *Blackberries or any other fresh berries can be used in place of the blueberries in this salad. Delicious served with wholegrain or rye bread.*

Serves 4

ingredients

250g/8oz watercress, broken into sprigs
I lettuce of your choice,
leaves separated
250g/8oz blueberries
250g/8oz yellow teardrop or red cherry
tomatoes, halved
I cucumber, seeded and chopped
<u>Passion Fruit Vinaigrette</u>
4 tablespoons passion fruit pulp
2 tablespoons white vinegar
I teaspoon sugar
2 teaspoons Dijon mustard
freshly ground black pepper

melon
in ginger syrup

Method:

1 Arrange watermelon, honeydew melon and rock melon (cantaloupe) on a serving platter. Cover and chill until required.

2 To make Ginger Syrup, place ginger, wine, sugar and lemon strips in a saucepan, bring to simmering over a medium heat and simmer, stirring occasionally, for 3 minutes. Transfer syrup to a bowl, cover and chill.

3 Just prior to serving, spoon syrup over melon.

Note: Use any combination of melons that are available for this recipe.

Serves 6-8

ingredients

**400g/12¹/₂oz watermelon,
cut into thick strips
300g/9¹/₂oz honeydew melon,
cut into thick strips
300g/9¹/₂oz rock melon (cantaloupe),
cut into thick strips**
<u>**Ginger syrup**</u>
**45g/1¹/₂oz preserved ginger in syrup,
thinly sliced
1 cup/250ml/8fl oz sweet ginger wine
2 tablespoons sugar
1 tablespoon thin lemon rind strips**

dressings

Salads and Dressings

Salads take only minutes to prepare and are delicious eaten as an accompaniment or as a light meal on their own. Dressings add interest to any salad or vegetable and the ones in this chapter are quick to make and can be kept in the refrigerator for a week or more.

Oriental Mayonnaise

2 tablespoons soft brown sugar
2 teaspoons grated fresh ginger
1 teaspoon fennel seeds
1 clove garlic, crushed
1/3 cup/90ml/3fl oz soy sauce
2 tablespoons cider vinegar
2 egg yolks
1/2 teaspoon dry mustard
3/4 cup/185ml/6 fl oz vegetable oil
2 teaspoons sesame oil
1/2 teaspoon hot chilli sauce

1 *Place sugar, ginger, fennel seeds, garlic, soy sauce and vinegar in a saucepan and bring to the boil. Reduce heat and simmer, uncovered, for 5 minutes or until mixture reduces by half. Remove from heat, strain and discard fennel seeds. Set aside to cool.*
2 *Place egg yolks and mustard in a food processor or blender and process until just combined. With machine running, gradually pour in vegetable and sesame oils and process until mayonnaise thickens.*
3 *Add soy mixture and process to combine. Mix in chilli sauce to taste.*
Note: *Store mayonnaise in a jar or bottle in the refrigerator for up to 1 week.*
Makes 1 1/2 cups/37ml/12fl oz

Mayonnaise

1/4 teaspoon dry mustard
2 egg yolks
1 cup/250ml/8fl oz olive oil
2 tablespoons lemon juice or white wine vinegar
freshly ground black pepper

Place mustard and egg yolks in a food processor or blender and process until just combined. With machine running, gradually pour in oil and process until mixture thickens. Blend in lemon juice or vinegar and black pepper to taste.

Green Herbed Mayonnaise: Purée

30g/1oz fresh basil leaves,
12 fresh chives,
2 tablespoons chopped fresh parsley and 1 clove garlic.

Prepare mayonnaise as above using vinegar rather than lemon juice. Stir basil purée into prepared mayonnaise.

Blue Cheese Mayonnaise: Crumble

90g/3oz blue cheese, add to prepared mayonnaise and process to combine.
Makes 1 1/2 cups/375ml/12fl oz

oils and vinegars

Ginger and Soy Dressing

1 tablespoon grated fresh ginger
1 clove garlic, crushed (optional)
1/2 cup/125ml/4fl oz soy sauce
1/2 cup/125ml/4fl oz water
1 tablespoon cider vinegar
1 tablespoon sesame oil

Place ginger, garlic (if using), soy sauce, water, vinegar and oil in a screwtop jar and shake well to combine. Stand for at least 15 minutes before using.
Note: *Store dressing in the jar in which you made it, in the refrigerator for 2-3 weeks. Shake well and bring to room temperature before using.*
Makes 1 cup/250ml/8fl oz

Basic Vinaigrette

3/4 cup/185ml/6fl oz olive oil
1/4 cup/60ml/2fl oz cider vinegar
1 tablespoon Dijon mustard
freshly ground black pepper

Place oil, vinegar, mustard and black pepper to taste in a screwtop jar and shake well to combine.

Walnut or Hazelnut Vinaigrette:

Replace olive oil with 3 tablespoons walnut or hazelnut oil and 1/2 cup/125ml/4fl oz vegetable oil.

Lemon Herb Vinaigrette:

Replace vinegar with lemon juice and add 60g/2oz mixed chopped fresh herbs such as basil, parsley, chives, rosemary, thyme or tarragon.
Note: *Store dressing in the jar in which you made it, in the refrigerator for 2-3 weeks. Shake well and bring to room temperature before using.*
Makes 1 cup/250ml/8fl oz

Yoghurt Dressing

2 tablespoons snipped fresh chives
1 clove garlic, crushed (optional)
3/4 cup/155g/5oz natural yoghurt
2 tablespoons white wine vinegar

1 *Place chives, garlic (if using), yoghurt and vinegar in a bowl and whisk to combine.*

Mint Yoghurt Dressing:

Prepare Yoghurt Dressing as described. Mix in 2 tablespoons finely chopped fresh mint.

Curried Yoghurt Dressing:

Prepare Yoghurt Dressing as described. Mix in 1 teaspoon curry powder and a dash of chilli sauce.

Thousand Island Yoghurt Dressing:

1 *Prepare Yoghurt Dressing as described, omitting garlic. Mix in 2 tablespoons chopped green olives, 2 finely chopped spring onions, 1 chopped hard-boiled egg, 1 tablespoon finely chopped green capsicum (pepper), 1 tablespoon tomato paste (purée) and 1/2 teaspoon chilli sauce.*
Note: *Store dressing in a screwtop jar in the refrigerator for up to 1 week.*
Makes 1 cup/250ml/8fl oz

Low-oil Vinaigrette

½ teaspoon dry mustard
⅔ cup/170ml/5½fl oz cider vinegar
⅓ cup/90ml/3fl oz olive oil
cayenne pepper
freshly ground black pepper

Place mustard, vinegar, oil and cayenne and black pepper to taste in a screwtop jar and shake well to combine.

Note: Store dressing in the jar in which you made it, in the refrigerator for 2-3 weeks. Shake well and bring to room temperature before using.

Makes 1 cup/250ml/8fl oz

Pesto Pasta Salad

45g/1½oz spiral pasta
4 cherry tomatoes, halved
1 slice leg ham, cut into thin strips
30g/1oz watercress or snow pea (mangetout) sprouts
__Pesto sauce__
15g/½oz fresh basil leaves
1 tablespoon pine nuts
1 clove garlic
2 tablespoons olive oil
1½ tablespoons grated Parmesan cheese
freshly ground black pepper

1 Cook pasta in boiling water in a saucepan following packet directions. Rinse under cold water, drain and set aside to cool.
2 To make sauce, place basil, pine nuts, garlic and 1 tablespoon oil in a food processor or blender and process until smooth. With machine running, gradually pour in remaining oil. Mix in Parmesan cheese and black pepper to taste.
3 Spoon sauce over pasta and toss to combine. Add tomatoes, ham and watercress or snow pea (mangetout) sprouts to salad and toss.

Note: This quantity is for a salad which is being served as a side dish, however it is also wonderful as a main course. To serve as a main course simply increase the pasta

quantity to 60-90g/2-3oz. It is also delicious served warm - keep the pasta warm after cooking and complete recipe as directed.

Makes 1 serving

Julienne Vegetable Salad

1 small carrot, cut into thin strips
1 small zucchini (courgette), cut into thin strips
½ stalk celery, cut into thin strips
__Ginger and Soy Dressing__
1 teaspoon sesame seeds, toasted

1 Arrange carrot, zucchini (courgette) and celery on a serving plate. Drizzle with dressing and sprinkle with sesame seeds.

Makes 1 serving

Simple Green Salad

4 small lettuce leaves
6 slices cucumber
¼ green capsicum (pepper), cut into thin strips
1 spring onion, finely chopped
1 teaspoon snipped fresh chives
1 teaspoon chopped fresh parsley
freshly ground black pepper
Basic Vinaigrette (page 75) or Low-oil Vinaigrette (page 76)

1 Arrange lettuce, cucumber, green capsicum (pepper) and spring onion on a serving plate. Scatter with chives and parsley and black pepper to taste. Drizzle with vinaigrette and serve immediately.

Note: Always dress a lettuce salad as close to serving time as possible. The longer a dressing sits on the leaves, the less crisp they will be.

Makes 1 serving

salads

Waldorf Salad

1 green or red apple, cored and sliced
1 teaspoon lemon juice
¹/₂ stalk celery, sliced
1 tablespoon roughly chopped walnuts
1¹/₂ tablespoons Mayonnaise (page 74)
or Yoghurt Dressing (page 75)
freshly ground black pepper

Place apple in a bowl, pour over lemon juice and toss to coat. Add celery, walnuts and mayonnaise or dressing and black pepper to taste and toss to combine.
Note: *Pecans or almonds are a tasty alternative to the walnuts in this easy salad.*
Makes 1 serving

Garden Salad

4 lettuce leaves, torn into pieces
4 cherry tomatoes or tomato wedges
4 button mushrooms, sliced
6 snow peas (mangetout)
or sugar snap peas
1 hard-boiled egg, cut into wedges
1 teaspoon chopped fresh parsley
1 teaspoon chopped fresh basil
2 teaspoons pine nuts, toasted
croûtons (see hint)
Mayonnaise (page 74) or
Yoghurt Dressing (page 75)

Arrange lettuce, tomatoes, mushrooms, snow peas (mangetout) or sugar snap peas and egg on a serving plate. Scatter with parsley, basil, pine nuts and croutons. Drizzle with a little mayonnaise or dressing and serve immediately.
Note: *To make croûtons, cut crusts from a slice of bread, then lightly brush with oil and cut into cubes. Place cubes on a baking tray and bake at 200°C/400°F/Gas 6 for 10-15 minutes or until croûtons are golden and crisp.*
Makes 1 serving.

Cooking is not an exact science: one does not require finely calibrated scales, pipettes and scientific equipment to cook, yet the conversion to metric measures in some countries and its interpretations must have intimidated many a good cook.

Weights are given in the recipes only for ingredients such as meats, fish, poultry and some vegetables. Though a few grams/ounces one way or another will not affect the success of your dish.

Though recipes have been tested using the Australian Standard 250ml cup, 20ml tablespoon and 5ml teaspoon, they will work just as well with the US and Canadian 8fl oz cup, or the UK 300ml cup. We have used graduated cup measures in preference to tablespoon measures so that proportions are always the same. Where tablespoon measures have been given, these are not crucial measures, so using the smaller tablespoon of the US or UK will not affect the recipe's success. At least we all agree on the teaspoon size.

For breads, cakes and pastries, the only area which might cause concern is where eggs are used, as proportions will then vary. If working with a 250ml or 300ml cup, use large eggs (60g/2oz), adding a little more liquid to the recipe for 300ml cup measures if it seems necessary. Use the medium-sized eggs (55g/1^1/4oz) with 8fl oz cup measure. A graduated set of measuring cups and spoons is recommended, the cups in particular for measuring dry ingredients. Remember to level such ingredients to ensure their accuracy.

English measures
All measurements are similar to Australian with two exceptions: the English cup measures 300mL/10fl oz, whereas the Australian cup measure 250mL/8fl oz. The English tablespoon (the Australian dessertspoon) measures 14.8ml/^{1}/2fl oz against the Australian tablespoon of 20ml/^{3}/4fl oz.

American measures
The American reputed pint is 16fl oz, a quart is equal to 32fl oz and the American gallon, 128fl oz. The Imperial measurement is 20fl oz to the pint, 40fl oz a quart and 160fl oz one gallon.

The American tablespoon is equal to 14.8ml/^{1}/2fl oz, the teaspoon is 5ml/^{1}/6fl oz. The cup measure is 250ml/8fl oz, the same as Australia.

Dry measures
All the measures are level, so when you have filled a cup or spoon, level it off with the edge of a knife. The scale below is the "cook's equivalent"; it is not an exact conversion of metric to imperial measurement. To calculate the exact metric equivalent yourself, use 2.2046 lb = 1kg or 1 lb = 0.45359kg

Metric		Imperial	
g = grams		oz = ounces	
kg = kilograms		lb = pound	
15g		^{1}/2oz	
20g		^{2}/3oz	
30g		1oz	
60g		2oz	
90g		3oz	
125g		4oz	^{1}/4 lb
155g		5oz	
185g		6oz	
220g		7oz	
250g		8oz	^{1}/2 lb
280g		9oz	
315g		10oz	
345g		11oz	
375g		12oz	^{3}/4 lb
410g		13oz	
440g		14oz	
470g		15oz	
1,000g	1kg	35.2oz	2.2 lb
	1.5kg		3.3 lb

Oven temperatures
The Celsius temperatures given here are not exact; they have been rounded off and are given as a guide only. Follow the manufacturer's temperature guide, relating it to oven description given in the recipe. Remember gas ovens are hottest at the top, electric ovens at the bottom and convection-fan forced ovens are usually even throughout. We included Regulo numbers for gas cookers which may assist. To convert °C to °F multiply °C by 9 and divide by 5 then add 32.

Oven temperatures

	C°	F°	Regulo
Very slow	120	250	1
Slow	150	300	2
Moderately slow	150	325	3
Moderate	180	350	4
Moderately hot	190-200	370-400	5-6
Hot	210-220	410-440	6-7
Very hot	230	450	8
Super hot	250-290	475-500	9-10

Cake dish sizes

Metric	Imperial
15cm	6in
18cm	7in
20cm	8in
23cm	9in

Loaf dish sizes

Metric	Imperial
23x12cm	9x5in
25x8cm	10x3in
28x18cm	11x7in

Liquid measures

Metric	Imperial	Cup & Spoon
ml	fl oz	
millilitres	fluid ounce	
5ml	1/6fl oz	1 teaspoon
20ml	2/3fl oz	1 tablespoon
30ml	1fl oz	1 tablespoon plus 2 teaspoons
60ml	2fl oz	1/4 cup
85ml	2 1/2fl oz	1/3 cup
100ml	3fl oz	3/8 cup
125ml	4fl oz	1/2 cup
150ml	5fl oz	1/4 pint, 1 gill
250ml	8fl oz	1 cup
300ml	10fl oz	1/2 pint)
360ml	12fl oz	1 1/2 cups
420ml	14fl oz	1 3/4 cups
500ml	16fl oz	2 cups
600ml	20fl oz 1 pint,	2 1/2 cups
1 litre	35fl oz 1 3/4 pints,	4 cups

Cup measurements

One cup is equal to the following weights.

	Metric	Imperial
Almonds, flaked	90g	3oz
Almonds, slivered, ground	125g	4oz
Almonds, kernel	155g	5oz
Apples, dried, chopped	125g	4oz
Apricots, dried, chopped	190g	6oz
Breadcrumbs, packet	125g	4oz

	Metric	Imperial
Breadcrumbs, soft	60g	2oz
Cheese, grated	125g	4oz
Choc bits	155g	5oz
Coconut, desiccated	90g	3oz
Cornflakes	30g	1oz
Currants	155g	5oz
Flour	125g	4oz
Fruit, dried (mixed, sultanas etc)	185g	6oz
Ginger, crystallised, glace	250g	8oz
Honey, treacle, golden syrup	315g	10oz
Mixed peel	220g	7oz
Nuts, chopped	125g	4oz
Prunes, chopped	220g	7oz
Rice, cooked	155g	5oz
Rice, uncooked	220g	7oz
Rolled oats	90g	3oz
Sesame seeds	125g	4oz
Shortening (butter, margarine)	250g	8oz
Sugar, brown	155g	5oz
Sugar, granulated or caster	250g	8oz
Sugar, sifted icing	155g	5oz
Wheatgerm	60g	2oz

Length

Some of us still have trouble converting imperial length to metric. In this scale, measures have been rounded off to the easiest-to-use and most acceptable figures.

To obtain the exact metric equivalent in converting inches to centimetres, multiply inches by 2.54 whereby 1 inch equals 25.4 millimetres and 1 millimetre equals 0.03937 inches.

Metric	Imperial
mm = millimetres	in = inches
cm = centimetres	ft = feet
5mm, 0.5cm	1/4in
10mm, 1.0cm	1/2in
20mm, 2.0cm	3/4in
2.5cm	1in
5cm	2in
8cm	3in
10cm	4in
12cm	5in
15cm	6in
18cm	7in
20cm	8in
23cm	9in
25cm	10in
28cm	11in
30cm	1 ft, 12in